Algonquin Area Public Library
2600 Harnish Dr.
Algonquin, IL 60102
www.aapld.org

Watch Me Go!

MY SKATES

Victor Blaine

PowerKiDS press.

New York

Published in 2015 by The Rosen Publishing Group, Inc.
29 East 21st Street, New York, NY 10010

First Edition

Editor: Sarah Machajewski
Book Design: Mickey Harmon

Photo Credits: Cover, p. 1 Adam Smith/The Image Bank/Getty Images; p. 5 Jacek Chabraszewski/Shutterstock.com; p. 6 (boy), 22 Kane Skennar/Digital Vision/Getty Images; p. 6 (in-line skates) Denys Kurylow/Shutterstock.com; p. 6 (quad-style skates) Mordechai Meiri/Shutterstock.com; p. 9 Suzy Hanzlik Photography/Moment Open/Getty Images; p. 10 NataSnow/Shutterstock.com; p. 13 Dima Chuck/Shutterstock.com; p. 14 Elena Yuksheva/Shutterstock.com; p. 17 2xSamara.com/Shutterstock.com; p. 18 Vladislav Gajic/Shutterstock.com; p. 21 Elena Elisseeva/Thinkstock.com.

Library of Congress Cataloging-in-Publication Data

Blaine, Victor.
My skates / by Victor Blaine.
p. cm. — (Watch me go!)
Includes index.
ISBN 978-1-4994-0256-8 (pbk.)
ISBN 978-1-4994-0239-1 (6-pack)
ISBN 978-1-4994-0254-4 (library binding)
1. In-line skating — Juvenile literature. 2. Roller skating — Juvenile literature. I. Title.
GV859.73 B53 2015
796.21—d23

Manufactured in the United States of America

CPSIA Compliance Information: Batch #CW15PK: For Further Information contact Rosen Publishing, New York, New York at 1-800-237-9932

CONTENTS

Have you ever gone skating?

There are two kinds of skates you can use.

Quad-style skates have four wheels. There are two wheels in front and two wheels in back.

In-line skates have four wheels, too. The wheels are in a straight line.

Most skates have **laces**. Laces keep the skates on your feet.

Skates make you move fast!
You must wear a **helmet**
in case you fall.

You can also wear **elbow pads** and **knee pads** to keep from getting hurt.

It's fun to skate outside. A place called a roller rink lets you skate inside.

Skating is fun on your own. It's also fun to skate with your friends.

People love to skate. What do you like about it?

WORDS TO KNOW

| elbow pad | helmet | knee pad | laces |

INDEX

H
helmet, 15

I
in-line skates, 11

K
knee pads, 16

Q
quad-style skates, 8

WEBSITES

Due to the changing nature of Internet links, PowerKids Press has developed an online list of websites related to the subject of this book. This site is updated regularly. Please use this link to access the list: www.powerkidslinks.com/wmg/skat